CW00400687

Quotable Dickens

QUOTABLE DICKENS

Summersdale Publishers Ltd
46 West Street
Chichester
West Sussex
PO19 1RP
UK

www.summersdale.com

Printed and bound in the Czech Republic

ISBN: 978-1-84953-258-7

Substantial discounts on bulk quantities of Summersdale books are available to corporations, professional associations and other organisations. For details telephone Summersdale Publishers on (+44-1243-771107), fax (+44-1243-786300) or email (nicky@summersdale.com).

Quotable

Dickens

summersdale

Contents

Love
and
Friendship

Love is in all things a most wonderful teacher...

Our Mutual Friend

Love, however, is very materially assisted by a warm and active imagination: which has a long memory, and will thrive, for a considerable time, on very slight and sparing food.

Nicholas Nickleby

'I hope that simple love
and truth will be strong in
the end. I hope that real
love and truth are stronger
in the end than any evil or
misfortune in the world.'

Agnes Wickfield, *David Copperfield*

Dombey and Son had often dealt in hides, but never in hearts. They left that fancy ware to boys and girls, and boarding-schools and books.

Dombey and Son

'I have been bent and broken, but – I hope – into a better shape. Be as considerate and good to me as you were, and tell me we are friends.'

Estella, *Great Expectations*

... she better liked to see him free and happy, even than to have him near her, because she loved him better than herself.

Mary Rudge on her son Barnaby, *Barnaby Rudge*

'It is, as Mr Rokesmith
says, a matter of feeling,
but Lor how many matters
ARE matters of feeling!'

Henrietta Boffin, *Our Mutual Friend*

Mystery and disappointment
are not absolutely
indispensable to the
growth of love, but
they are, very often, its
powerful auxiliaries.

Nicholas Nickleby

'There can be no disparity in marriage like unsuitability of mind and purpose.'

Mrs Markleham, *David Copperfield*

'You know me. It's my old girl that advises. She has the head. But I never own to it before her. Discipline must be maintained.'

Matthew Bagnet, *Bleak House*

Love, though said to be afflicted with blindness, is a vigilant watchman...

Our Mutual Friend

Miss Mills replied, on general principles, that the Cottage of content was better than the Palace of cold splendour, and that where love was, all was.

David Copperfield

Her look at her father, half admiring him and proud of him, half ashamed for him, all devoted and loving, went to his inmost heart.

Little Dorrit

'I wish you could make a friend
of me, Lizzie. Do you think
you could? I have no more of
what they call character, my
dear, than a canary-bird, but
I know I am trustworthy.'

Bella Wilfer, *Our Mutual Friend*

Human Nature

*He is an honourable,
obstinate, truthful,
high-spirited, intensely
prejudiced, perfectly
unreasonable man.*

On Sir Leicester Dedlock, *Bleak House*

'He is quite a good
fellow – nobody's
enemy but his own.'

Mr Waterbrook on Tommy Traddles, *David Copperfield*

'Why am I always at war
with myself? Why have I
told, as if upon compulsion,
what I knew all along I
ought to have withheld?'

Bella Wilfer, *Our Mutual Friend*

... in the majority of cases, conscience is an elastic and very flexible article, which will bear a deal of stretching and adapt itself to a great variety of circumstances.

The Old Curiosity Shop

'Subdue your appetites,
my dears, and you've
conquered human nature.'

Wackford Squeers, *Nicholas Nickleby*

All other swindlers upon earth are nothing to the self-swindlers, and with such pretences did I cheat myself. Surely a curious thing.

Great Expectations

'There is no deception now, Mr Weller. Tears,' said Job, with a look of momentary slyness, 'tears are not the only proofs of distress, nor the best ones.'

Job Trotter, *The Pickwick Papers*

Strong mental agitation and disturbance was no novelty to him, even before his late sufferings. It never is, to obstinate and sullen natures; for they struggle hard to be such.

Dombey and Son

'Mrs Boffin and me, ma'am, are plain people, and we don't want to pretend to anything, nor yet to go round and round at anything because there's always a straight way to everything.'

Noddy Boffin, *Our Mutual Friend*

'It is a principle of his that no man who was not a true gentleman at heart, ever was, since the world began, a true gentleman in manner.'

Herbert Pocket on his father, Matthew Pocket, *Great Expectations*

'My meaning is, that no man
can expect his children to
respect what he degrades.'

Tom Pinch, Martin Chuzzlewit

*If our affections be tried, our
affections are our consolation
and comfort; and memory,
however sad, is the best
and purest link between
this world and a better.*

Nicholas Nickleby

But his power is very great, notwithstanding; and the dignity of his office is never impaired by the absence of efforts on his part to maintain it.

On the parish beadle, *Sketches by Boz*

Anything that makes a noise
is satisfactory to a crowd.

The Old Curiosity Shop

Lawyers hold that there are two kinds of particularly bad witnesses – a reluctant witness, and a too-willing witness; it was Mr Winkle's fate to figure in both characters.

The Pickwick Papers

'A truly refined mind will seem to be ignorant of the existence of anything that is not perfectly proper, placid, and pleasant.'

Mrs General, *Little Dorrit*

In a word, I was too
cowardly to do what I knew
to be right, as I had been
too cowardly to avoid doing
what I knew to be wrong.

Great Expectations

Quadruped lions are said to be savage, only when they are hungry; biped lions are rarely sulky longer than when their appetite for distinction remains unappeased.

Nicholas Nickleby

*It is one of the easiest
achievements in life
to offend your family
when your family want
to get rid of you.*

Our Mutual Friend

... he had everything but any touch of nature; he was not like youth, he was not like age, he was not like anything in the world but a model of deportment.

On Mr Turveydrop, *Bleak House*

Filthy
Lucre

*Gold, for the instant,
lost its lustre in his eyes,
for there were countless
treasures of the heart which
it could never purchase.*

Nicholas Nickleby

*Darkness is cheap, and
Scrooge liked it.*

A Christmas Carol

'A man can well afford
to be as bold as brass,
my good fellow, when he
gets gold in exchange!'

Montague Tigg, *Martin Chuzzlewit*

'A person who can't pay,
gets another person who
can't pay, to guarantee
that he can pay.'

Mr Pancks, *Little Dorrit*

... for gold conjures up a mist about a man, more destructive of all his old senses and lulling to his feelings than the fumes of charcoal...

Nicholas Nickleby

'Here's the rule for bargains – "Do other men, for they would do you." That's the true business precept. All others are counterfeits.'

Jonas Chuzzlewit, *Martin Chuzzlewit*

'Blood cannot be obtained
from a stone, neither can
anything on account be
obtained at present (not
to mention law expenses)
from Mr Micawber.'

Emma Micawber, David Copperfield

The civility which money will purchase, is rarely extended to those who have none...

Sketches by Boz

*It is a melancholy truth
that even great men have
their poor relations.
Indeed great men have
often more than their fair
share of poor relations...*

Bleak House

'I am a demd villain!' cried Mr Mantalini, smiting himself on the head. 'I will fill my pockets with change for a sovereign in halfpence and drown myself in the Thames...'

Nicholas Nickleby

'Rich folks may ride
on camels, but it an't
so easy for 'em to see
out of a needle's eye.
That is my comfort, and
I hope I knows it.'

Sarah Gamp, Martin Chuzzlewit

Hope
and
Happiness

'I am as light as a feather,
I am as happy as an
angel, I am as merry as a
school-boy. I am as giddy
as a drunken man.'

Ebenezer Scrooge, A Christmas Carol

The flowers that sleep by night, opened their gentle eyes and turned them to the day. The light, creation's mind, was everywhere, and all things owned its power.

The Old Curiosity Shop

'Wait a moment, and I'll go on with the lecture. Give me a moment, because I like to cry for joy. It's so delicious, John dear, to cry for joy.'

Bella Wilfer, *Our Mutual Friend*

It is a fair, even-handed, noble adjustment of things, that while there is infection in disease and sorrow, there is nothing in the world so irresistibly contagious as laughter and good-humour.

A Christmas Carol

... his nerves were rendered stouter and more vigorous, by showers of tears, which, being tokens of weakness, and so far tacit admissions of his own power, pleased and exalted him.

On Mr Bumble, *Oliver Twist*

'We are not rich in the bank, but we have always prospered, and we have quite enough. I never walk out with my husband but I hear the people bless him.'

Esther Summerson, *Bleak House*

'Walter,' she said, looking
full upon him with her
affectionate eyes, 'like you,
I hope for better things.
I will pray for them, and
believe that they will arrive.'

Florence Dombey, *Dombey and Son*

'Always hope; that's a dear boy. Never leave off hoping; it don't answer. Do you mind me, Nick? It don't answer. Don't leave a stone unturned.'

Newman Noggs, *Nicholas Nickleby*

'Can you suppose there's
any harm in looking
as cheerful and being
as cheerful as our poor
circumstances will permit?'

Kit Nubbles, *The Old Curiosity Shop*

'Something will come
of this. I hope it mayn't
be human gore!'

Simon Tappertit, *Barnaby Rudge*

'Ah, Miss, hope is an excellent thing for such as has the spirits to bear it!'

Mrs Wickam, *Dombey and Son*

*... and from the death
of each day's hope
another hope sprung
up to live to-morrow.*

The Old Curiosity Shop

Darker Musings

There are dark shadows
on the earth, but its lights
are stronger in the contrast.
Some men, like bats or owls,
have better eyes for the
darkness than for the light.

The Pickwick Papers

Captain Cuttle, like all mankind, little knew how much hope had survived within him under discouragement, until he felt its death-shock.

Dombey and Son

So, throughout life, our worst weaknesses and meannesses are usually committed for the sake of the people whom we most despise.

Great Expectations

So do the shadows of our own desires stand between us and our better angels, and thus their brightness is eclipsed.

Barnaby Rudge

'A spirit that was once
a man could hardly feel
stranger or lonelier, going
unrecognised among
mankind, than I feel.'

John Rokesmith, *Our Mutual Friend*

'When you say you love me,
I know what you mean,
as a form of words; but
nothing more. You address
nothing in my breast, you
touch nothing there.'

Estella, *Great Expectations*

'As I said just now, the world has gone past me. I don't blame it; but I no longer understand it.'

Solomon Gills, *Dombey and Son*

The smoke hung sluggishly above the chimney-tops as if it lacked the courage to rise, and the rain came slowly and doggedly down, as if it had not even the spirit to pour.

The Pickwick Papers

Surprises, like misfortunes,
seldom come alone.

Oliver Twist

I was always treated as if I had insisted on being born in opposition to the dictates of reason, religion, and morality, and against the dissuading arguments of my best friends.

Great Expectations

Death, self-interest, and fortune's changes, are every day breaking up many a happy group, and scattering them far and wide; and the boys and girls never come back again.

The Pickwick Papers

'Circumstances may accumulate so strongly even against an innocent man, that directed, sharpened, and pointed, they may slay him.'

John Jasper, *The Mystery of Edwin Drood*

'Have I yet to learn that
the hardest and best-borne
trials are those which are
never chronicled in any
earthly record, and are
suffered every day!'

Mr Marton, *The Old Curiosity Shop*

'It's over, and can't be helped, and that's one consolation, as they always says in Turkey, ven they cuts the wrong man's head off.'

Sam Weller, *The Pickwick Papers*

When I was left in this
way, I used to sit, think,
think, thinking, till I felt
as lonesome as a kitten
in a wash-house copper
with the lid on...

Sketches by Boz

'He'd no more heart
than a iron file, he was
as cold as death, and
he had the head of the
Devil afore mentioned.'

Provis (Abel Magwitch) on Compeyson, *Great Expectations*

A
Sense of
Humour

'She has produced some delightful pieces, herself, sir. You may have met with her "Ode to an Expiring Frog," sir.'

Leo Hunter, *The Pickwick Papers*

Can I view thee panting, lying
On thy stomach,
without sighing;
Can I unmoved see thee dying
On a log
Expiring frog!

Mrs Leo Hunter, 'Ode to an Expiring Frog',
The Pickwick Papers

'If there is a word in the dictionary under any letter from A to Z that I abominate, it is energy. It is such a conventional superstition, such parrot gabble!'

Eugene Wrayburn, *Our Mutual Friend*

'I shouldn't wish it to be mentioned, but it's a' – here he beckoned to me, and put his lips close to my ear – 'it's a mad world. Mad as Bedlam, boy!'

Mr Dick (Richard Babley), *David Copperfield*

'Cows are my passion.
What I have ever sighed
for, has been to retreat
to a Swiss farm, and live
entirely surrounded by
cows – and china.'

Cleopatra Skewton, *Dombey and Son*

'Think! I've got enough
to do, and little enough
to get for it without
thinking. Thinking!'

Coavinses (Mr Neckett), *Bleak House*

'Battledore and shuttlecock's a wery good game, vhen you ain't the shuttlecock and two lawyers the battledores, in which case it gets too excitin' to be pleasant.'

Sam Weller, *The Pickwick Papers*

'Was it her hairdresser who had escaped from a bear, or was it a bear who had escaped from her hairdresser's? I declare I can't remember just now.'

Mrs Nickleby, *Nicholas Nickleby*

'A literary man – WITH
a wooden leg – and all
Print is open to him!'

Noddy Boffin on Silas Wegg, *Our Mutual Friend*

'We hope to have, before long,
a board of fact, composed of
commissioners of fact, who will
force the people to be a people
of fact, and of nothing but fact.'

The Government Officer, *Hard Times*

*'Oh gracious, why wasn't
I born old and ugly!'*

Miss Miggs, *Barnaby Rudge*

'It's a pleasant world we live
in sir, a very pleasant world.
There are bad people in it, Mr
Richard, but if there were no
bad people, there would be
no good lawyers. Ha ha!'

Sampson Brass, *The Old Curiosity Shop*

Barnacle junior stared at him until his eye-glass fell out, and then put it in again and stared at him until it fell out again.

Little Dorrit

'... *there are only two styles of portrait painting; the serious and the smirk.*'

Miss La Creevy, *Nicholas Nickleby*

'Poetry's unnat'ral;
no man ever talked
poetry 'cept a beadle on
boxin'-day, or Warren's
blackin', or Rowland's oil, or
some of them low fellows.'

Tony Weller, *The Pickwick Papers*

'There is no such passion
in human nature, as the
passion for gravy among
commercial gentlemen.'

Mrs Todgers, *Martin Chuzzlewit*

Strength
in
Adversity

'Then tell Wind and Fire
where to stop,' returned
madame; 'but don't tell me.'

Madame Defarge, *A Tale of Two Cities*

He was bolder in the daylight – most men are.

On Tom Smart, *The Pickwick Papers*

'No man knows till the time comes, what depths are within him. To some men it never comes; let them rest and be thankful!'

Bradley Headstone, *Our Mutual Friend*

'... although the happiness
and delight of my life lie
buried there too, I have not
made a coffin of my heart,
and sealed it up, forever,
on my best affections.'

Mr Brownlow, *Oliver Twist*

'I don't profess to be profound; but I do lay claim to common sense.'

Jane Murdstone, *David Copperfield*

In that giddy whirl of noise and confusion, the men were delirious. Who thought of money, ruin, or the morrow, in the savage intoxication of the moment?

Nicholas Nickleby

'You might, from your appearance, be the wife of Lucifer,' said Miss Pross, in her breathing. 'Nevertheless, you shall not get the better of me. I am an Englishwoman.'

A Tale of Two Cities

*Whether I shall turn out to
be the hero of my own life,
or whether that station will
be held by anybody else,
these pages must show.*

David Copperfield

'You will profit by the failure, and will avoid it another time. I have done a similar thing myself, in construction, often. Every failure teaches a man something, if he will learn; and you are too sensible a man not to learn from this failure.'

Daniel Doyce, *Little Dorrit*

However, the Sun himself is weak when he first rises, and gathers strength and courage as the day gets on.

The Old Curiosity Shop

'The men who learn
endurance, are they who call
the whole world, brother.'

Geoffrey Haredale, *Barnaby Rudge*

*She was truest to them
in the season of trial, as
all the quietly loyal and
good will always be.*

On Lucie Manette, *A Tale of Two Cities*

'My daughter, there are times of moral danger when the hardest virtuous resolution to form is flight, and when the most heroic bravery is flight.'

Mr Riah, *Our Mutual Friend*

'But if I have a girl's weakness, I have a woman's heart, and it is not you who in a cause like this can turn that from its purpose.'

Kate Nickleby, *Nicholas Nickleby*

'I've been done everything to, pretty well – except hanged. I've been locked up as much as a silver tea-kittle.'

Provis (Abel Magwitch), *Great Expectations*

'The object of our lives is won. Henceforth let us wear it silently. My lips are closed upon the past from this hour. I forgive you your part in to-morrow's wickedness.'

Edith Granger, *Dombey and Son*

'It is a far, far better thing
that I do, than I have
ever done; it is a far, far
better rest that I go to
than I have ever known.'

Sydney Carton, A Tale of Two Cities

Philosophical Thoughts

*... the old year was preparing,
like an ancient philosopher,
to call his friends around
him, and amidst the sound of
feasting and revelry to pass
gently and calmly away.*

The Pickwick Papers

*Look round and round upon
this bare bleak plain, and see
even here, upon a winter's day,
how beautiful the shadows
are! Alas! it is the nature
of their kind to be so.*

Martin Chuzzlewit

*I had considered how the
things that never happen,
are often as much realities
to us, in their effects, as
those that are accomplished.*

David Copperfield

'Death doesn't change us
more than life, my dear.'

Old Woman, *The Old Curiosity Shop*

'It's nothing,' returned
Mrs Chick, 'It's merely
change of weather. We
must expect change.'

Louisa Chick, *Dombey and Son*

'*Take nothing on its looks;
take everything on evidence.
There's no better rule.*'

Mr Jaggers, *Great Expectations*

No one who can read,
ever looks at a book,
even unopened on a shelf,
like one who cannot.

Our Mutual Friend

The sun does not shine upon this fair earth to meet frowning eyes, depend upon it.

Nicholas Nickleby

'Lord bless you!' said Mr
Omer, resuming his pipe,
'a man must take the
fat with the lean; that's
what he must make up
his mind to, in this life.'

David Copperfield

'Some persons hold,' he
pursued, still hesitating,
'that there is a wisdom of
the Head, and that there is
a wisdom of the Heart.'

Thomas Gradgrind, *Hard Times*

It is not easy to walk alone in the country without musing upon something.

Little Dorrit

'I only ask to be free. The butterflies are free. Mankind will surely not deny to Harold Skimpole what it concedes to the butterflies!'

Harold Skimpole, *Bleak House*

*Time and tide will wait
for no man, saith the
adage. But all men have
to wait for time and tide.*

Martin Chuzzlewit

... for your popular rumour, unlike the rolling stone of the proverb, is one which gathers a deal of moss in its wanderings up and down...

The Old Curiosity Shop

I think of every little trifle between me and Dora, and feel the truth, that trifles make the sum of life.

David Copperfield

'... you have my word; and
how you can have that, without
my honour too, I don't know.
I've sorted a lot of dust in my
time, but I never knew the two
things go into separate heaps.'

Noddy Boffin, *Our Mutual Friend*

... Father Time is not always a hard parent, and, though he tarries for none of his children, often lays his hand lightly upon those who have used him well...

Barnaby Rudge

Never wonder. By means of addition, subtraction, multiplication, and division, settle everything somehow, and never wonder.

Hard Times

'I take it as it comes, and make the most of it. That's the best way, ain't it?'

Mr Omer, *David Copperfield*

*Reflect upon your present
blessings – of which every
man has many – not on
your past misfortunes, of
which all men have some.*

Sketches by Boz

'Pip, dear old chap, life
is made of ever so many
partings welded together...'

Joe Gargery, *Great Expectations*

Wicked Wit

*Of an ungainly make
was Sloppy. Too much of
him longwise, too little
of him broadwise, and
too many sharp angles
of him angle-wise.*

Our Mutual Friend

... everybody seemed to eat his utmost in self-defence, as if a famine were expected to set in before breakfast time to-morrow morning...

Martin Chuzzlewit

Mr Chadband is a large
yellow man with a fat smile
and a general appearance
of having a good deal of
train oil in his system.

Bleak House

'I know quite enough of myself,'
said Bella, with a charming air
of being inclined to give herself
up as a bad job, 'and I don't
improve upon acquaintance.'

Bella Wilfer, *Our Mutual Friend*

*Affery, like greater people,
had always been right
in her facts, and always
wrong in the theories she
deduced from them.*

Little Dorrit

'Well, if I knew as little
of life as that, I'd eat
my hat and swallow the
buckle whole,' said the
clerical gentleman.

The Pickwick Papers

... his philanthropy was of that gunpowderous sort that the difference between it and animosity was hard to determine.

On Mr Honeythunder, *The Mystery of Edwin Drood*

'Your sex have such a surprising animosity against one another when you do differ.'

Inspector Bucket, *Bleak House*

'My pa requests me to
write to you, the doctors
considering it doubtful
whether he will ever recuvver
the use of his legs which
prevents his holding a pen.'

Fanny Squeers, *Nicholas Nickleby*

Mrs Varden was a lady of what is commonly called an uncertain temper – a phrase which being interpreted signifies a temper tolerably certain to make everybody more or less uncomfortable.

Barnaby Rudge

His family is as old as the hills,
and infinitely more respectable.
He has a general opinion
that the world might get on
without hills but would be
done up without Dedlocks.

On Sir Leicester Dedlock, *Bleak House*

Mr Podsnap was well to do, and stood very high in Mr Podsnap's opinion.

Our Mutual Friend

Much vexed by this reflection, Mr Squeers looked at the little boy to see whether he was doing anything he could beat him for.

Nicholas Nickleby

'Do you mean to say,
child, that any human
being has gone into a
Christian church, and got
herself named Peggotty?'

Betsey Trotwood, *David Copperfield*

*... a short, shrewd niece,
something too violently
compressed about the waist,
and with a sharp nose like a
sharp autumn evening, inclining
to be frosty towards the end.*

On Mr Snagsby's niece, *Bleak House*

From Twemlow's, Veneering
dashes at Podsnap's place
of business. Finds Podsnap
reading the paper, standing, and
inclined to be oratorical over
the astonishing discovery he has
made, that Italy is not England.

Our Mutual Friend

*Mr Squeers's appearance
was not prepossessing.
He had but one eye, and
the popular prejudice
runs in favour of two.*

Nicholas Nickleby

www.summersdale.com